MY FEELINGS

Books by Nick Flynn

NICK FLYNN

MY FEELINGS

POEMS

Graywolf Press

This publication is made possible, in part, by the voters of Minnesota through a Minnesota State Arts Board Operating Support grant, thanks to a legislative appropriation from the arts and cultural heritage fund, and through grants from the National Endowment for the Arts and the Wells Fargo Foundation Minnesota. Significant support has also been provided by Target, the McKnight Foundation, Amazon.com, and other generous contributions from foundations, corporations, and individuals. To these organizations and individuals we offer our heartfelt thanks.

Disclaimer: The word "my" in the title is meant to signify the author—as such no claims are made on anyone else's.

Published by Graywolf Press
250 Third Avenue North, Suite 600
Minneapolis, Minnesota 55401

www.graywolfpress.org

Published in the United States of America

ISBN 978-1-55597-710-8

2 4 6 8 9 7 5 3 1
First Graywolf Printing, 2015

Library of Congress Control Number: 2014960044

Cover design: Kapo Ng

Cover art: Lori Nix, *Laundromat.*

for jeff shotts

MY FEELINGS

You cannot fold a Flood—
And put it in a Drawer—

MY FEELINGS

BELLY OF THE BEAST

Here again
at the edge of what was,

the river held back
by the stones it has carried,

the knife in your hand
brimming

rain. Inside this day
without beginning or end, it cannot

stand still inside you.

One day I'll leave—not you
but all this—this hunger

that pushes each wave.

AK-47

1

love lays hold of everything

2

& *yes* all the houses whiten in the sun just as they whiten *yes* in the snow & *yes* from above each looks like a tombstone *yes* just as a graveyard from above is a city *yes* the world is one big graveyard after all

3

a phone rings in a labyrinth

4

this house, unpainted still—when you go back, if you go back, if you can find your way, it won't, it cannot *[your hand on the door]* be as you remember . . .

5

what need is there to build a labyrinth when [your hand on the door] *the entire universe is one?*

6

the amnesiac in the film last night tattooed words on his body—*november. ohio. rain*—to remember he was grieving his dead wife

7

this house you grew out of you grew up inside it

8

it lays hold of everything, it tears the top off a mountain, calls it *volcano*, pulls out the ore, lays it in fire, forges it with its hammer—it can be shaped into anything

9

inside this house a gun was cocked, uncocked, picked up, put down, aimed, lowered

10

a phone rings in a labyrinth, the dealer taps the tip of his blade to your heart *[surely we have been born for a reason]*—see how his mouth opens to let the words out, words we cannot see, his mouth as dark as alpha centauri

11

ALPHA: the first
CENTAURI: warrior
YOU: a small part of this unending
MOUTH: light seeps from inside you

12

the amnesiac's days are reduced to tracking down the man who killed his wife but the story is told backward & the more we see the more it seems that this is just the story he tells himself, that he cannot even remember his wife, the wires are crossed, maybe he is the one who killed her & now he is using vengeance as the engine to drive his body through time

13

& *yes* each of us is born with a gun on the wall *yes* a gun in the closet *yes* a gun to our heads—you cannot say it has always been this way but it has been this way for a long *yes* a long long time & this way it is now

14

& each face melts one into another as the gun is passed hand to melting hand, always held, always in someone's hand, the same gun in different hands or different guns in one hand, aimed or shot or raised over her head after the shot

15

& eye for eye & dust to dust the cartridges line up—each a word you must utter

16

& the path each bullet makes through the air means only one thing: *I am I am I am I am I am I am*

17

a phone rings in a labyrinth *[this is a metaphor for the past]*

18

think *blood oath*   think *suffering*   think *revenge*
think *I'm sick of doing one thing*   & *missing another*
think *the hard O of its mouth*   think *at least this is something*
at least I can hold it   think *whatever abstraction you can*
insert here _____   *a tunnel to crawl inside*

19

we could melt it down *[could we?]* into nails or bells or railroad
tracks or a tin cup or a steel toe or a spool of wire or a shovel
or a leg brace or a ladder or a bedpan or scaffolding or a sewing
needle or a typewriter or a hammer or a crutch or brake pads
or a tiny crucifix

20

see how the mouth opens to let the moth out *[they always fly into
the light]*—this might after all be necessary—we cannot know
what change will blossom, what will become, we cannot know
if each bullet is not a seed

21

to love the dead is endless tears

22

I don't know why god keeps blessing me

23

only silence is perfect

KAFKA

The cause of death seems to have been
starvation—his throat closed

& so he was no longer able to swallow. On his
deathbed he was editing *The Hunger*

Artist, which, perhaps ironically (perhaps
not), he'd begun working on before he was

felled. My father

will, the doctor tells me, also starve to death,
he also cannot swallow I have said no

to the feeding tube because I imagine that is
what I would want someone to say for me,

but really, how the fuck do I know? The fact

that I am the one who will pull the plug on him
& that I will pull it with one simple word

is in the realm of the unbearable, but
apparently

I will bear it. The doctor promises to make him
comfortable, which means

morphine . . . nowadays this is how the plug
is pulled. Afterward,

the money he buried under that tree,
the take from all his bank jobs, all of it

will come to me, if I can just get him to draw me
a map, if I can find the tree, if I can find

his shovel. And the house, the mansion he
grew up in, soon a lawyer will pass

a key across a walnut desk, but even this
lawyer will not be able to tell me where this

mansion is. And my father's masterpieces, his
many novels, mine

now to publish—I don't have to tell anyone
I didn't write them, not a word.

THE WHEN & THE HOW

A few days into it   *extravagant subterranean*
mystifying   as we walked from the L back to

my apartment   *inappropriate dormant*
complicated   I asked about your family—you

(like me) had yet to mention any   *desperate distant*
tethered

& as the question left my mouth I knew

confusing tongue-tied   the instant before you
spoke it   *incomprehensible wayworn insubstantial*

the moment I conjured her   *shadowy mystical*
elemental

by uttering the word MOTHER   *fucked-up*

painful wounded invisible unspeakable meaningless
I knew yours (like mine) had killed herself *delicate* & that

desperate unknown   our conversations
from that moment on would be simply   *broken*

limited backwoods

a matter of the how   *flimsy shameful crushing*
& the when

forbidden closeted
which would matter only in so far as

all-encompassing epic god-given

it would let me know something of your struggle
phantom oceanic flickering   & you

uncontainable feral misguided
something of mine

TANTALUS

From the piss on the bark, from the ash on
the leaf, from the scar

you pass on, from the cross you carve deep,
nothing here falls

you haven't let fall, air snatched from the buck
mid-leap. His flesh will pass through you

as you pass through your sons—
should have eaten them

when they were tiny.

BEADS OF SWEAT

Blind drunk, crank drunk,
blind to suffering, blind to joy—

please
let me begin again. Even

Moses, that day he went up
that mountain

to hear how from that day on it must

be, even Moses couldn't look, not for
long, into what we call still *unknowable*,

still *unsayable*, still *whirlwind*, still
       abyss . . . Up there he heard

a voice, *When I speak you will know*
from where it comes

& you will turn into it. I've been
trying, wandering this earth

for five years now, wandering the way a river
tells us it's alive

by the feather on its surface that cannot stop
moving. Each night

my father points to his bandaged
wrist—he is no more than

the sounds he makes now. *I know*

who you are, he says, *of course I know,* but he
doesn't, not really—he never was

infinite, I

know that now. Ride with me
when I go to him—someone will

have to let us in, someone who knows
the code. He won't complain—there

someone always picks you up when you
fall, someone

brings you juice. One floor above is
abandoned—can we still call it heaven? A line

of starlings on a telephone wire outside
his window, their shadows so small beneath them,

as small as you & I, balanced on our own
shadows—we do not fall, no one is falling,

the tire beneath us

gyroscopic—*clockwise forward, clockwise
tomorrow, clockwise*

gone. Moses was offered a glimpse
of what? *God's ass? Eternity?*

& it blinded him forever. Who
can tell me where I will fall next, where

the thorn will enter?

AQUARIUM

                                        Imagine
an aquarium, one fish inside, slowly circling.
Imagine two cameras set up to film this

aquarium, to film this one fish . . . *Is it a clown fish?*
A clown fish? Sure, a clown fish. Imagine also

you are unable to see this aquarium directly, it is in
another room & you don't know where that room

is. You are in your room, watching a screen,
the clown fish swims on that screen in that faraway

aquarium—a box within a box, a glass

                                within a glass. Think
of the cars we used to drive, no more than two
couches on wheels—we'd drink & drive & park

& make out, we had nowhere else to be. Our girls
were named Mary & Mary—it was a Catholic town—

& we'd watch each other move over & through them
& they, moving, watched us, a dim light buried in

the ceiling far above. Sometimes I'd catch Mary's
eye, but not my Mary. It wasn't as bad as you might
imagine—

we'd share whatever pills we'd swiped from our moms'
medicine chests, we'd grind them up & snort them if
there wasn't enough

& there was never enough. Now remember that
aquarium, those cameras, that room you will never

enter—the screen is split

so it seems you are watching two fish, but it is only
one. One fish turns, the other turns at the same

moment, synchronized, as if they are talking to
each other, as if they knew—this, the scientists

assert, is happening all the time—we are in a room,
watching the day unfold, but we have no idea

how many cameras are set up. One fish swims

inside its tiny ocean—Mary smiles at Mary, not
at me. We think this world must be broken into

fragments, we think memories are dispersed
throughout the brain & that the brain itself is

dispersed. We

think we began from a bang, but the bang never
stopped. Mary watches

Mary, waiting to see what will happen—the night
has to end somewhere. *Communion.* Communion

is the word.

FATHER, INSECT

After her
bath, as a way to apologize for all

my imperfections, I remind my
daughter, *You know, before you were*

born, I was not

a father. She takes this in
silently, moving a tiny blue elephant across

the rug. *If you weren't a father,* she
eventually asks, *then what were you—*

a bug? We'd been looking at pictures
of cavemen, talking

about evolution, about where we
came from, about all those

who came before—*Are they us?*
she asks. I

tell her about the carbon in her
pencil, about hydrogen bonding

with oxygen, about bacteria with
only one thought in their tiny

heads—she

uses her finger to write it all out
in the air, creating each

word as I speak it. When
did want become more

than hunger, when

did need become more
than shadow? Ecclesiastes warns

about the making

of books, of which there is no end,
this chain of meaning, this

offering—the book we both will write
today into today into today.

MY TRIGGERS

Hers: buildings, windows, department stores (her mother had thrown her body from one). Mine: pills, guns, the ocean (mine tried each before succeeding). This was the how. The when for us was the same—*autumn*—we'd go inside ourselves every fall & neither was in any shape to look for the other, to coax the other back, not really. Her mother hadn't left a note, mine had written I FEEL TOO MUCH in hers, over & over, as if these unnamed feelings, *as indispensible as oxygen for the body,* could destroy her (they did). We never discussed the why.

MY JOKE

As I put the pipe to my lips
As I lift the flame to the glass

My joke

As the smoke fills me: *Say good-bye to
Nick,* even if

I am the only one in the room
& by the end I was always

The only one in the room.

WHEN I WAS A GIRL

When I was a girl, climbing outside my
body, every eye I

felt, my legs no longer
mine. A circle

of boys, a circle of girls . . . Let's
play *Slave*, one said—I'll be *Master*, you

be *Yard Boss*, you can do

my whipping for me. If I
want the rest to carry me they will

carry me—I will make

a moving throne of their
bodies. Look here, this one has

a good set of teeth, I will call her
Nursemaid, she will live in my

mansion, I will come in the night. *Yes*,
she will say, yes, as I write everything out

on her back. When I

was a girl no one kissed outside of
a word, but the word

couldn't be *kiss,* or *lips,* or *tongue,*
the word had to point to something

outside us—an ant, say, carrying
a leaf—that

was the game. When I was a girl I'd
strap one on, she'd look over her

shoulder, I could make her

smile. *Find me*
as I'm falling, I'd whisper. Geologists

now claim that the ocean is fed by
an invisible ocean, a crystal at

the center of the earth. It

waits, not as vapor, not as liquid, not
as ice, but crystal, an enormous

jewel, waiting
to open. So much I don't understand. In

the beginning
girls ran across burning fields

with swords made of sticks; girls
hid in trees, stones heavy in their

hands. In the beginning I was

a girl, I held out my hand & it filled with
sunlight. If a bird landed in my palm

I could either crush it
or set it free.

HARBOR

If this bowl is always empty
If it breathes   if it's lung
If a horse can rise from the ashes

Saul was a sailor on the boat to Damascus
He did not know what he was
Paul turned to a voice   it rose up from the waves
It chained his boat to the darkness

A man finds ash   & he makes it a man
A horse finds ash in a horse
It lifts us   it holds us   it breaks us again
It scatters us into the harbor

[three]

CATHEDRAL OF SALT

Beneath all this I'm carving a cathedral
of salt. I keep

the entrance hidden, no one seems to notice
the hours I'm missing . . . I'll

bring you one night, it's where I
go when I

hang up the phone . . .

                Neither you
nor your soul is waiting for me at

the end of this, I know that now, the salt
nearly clear after I

chisel out the pews, the see-through
altar, the opaque

panels that depict the stations of
our cross—*Here is the day*

we met, here is the day we remember we
met . . . The air down here

will kill us, some say, some wear paper
masks, some still imagine the air above the green

trees, thick with bees

building solitary nests out of petals. What's
the name for that? *Ineffable?* The endless

white will blind you, some say,
but what is there to see we haven't already

seen? Some say it's like
poking a stick into a river—you might as well

simply write about the stick.
Or the river.

MY BLINDNESS

                              Is it today
I finally stand on the lunch counter

& ask for a moment of silence for the still
sick & suffering both in & out of my

mind? Is it today you finally open your shirt

enough to show me the collarbone
your heart hangs from? A man

is defined as one who "pisseth against
the wall." Lilith

objected to having to lie beneath Adam but Adam
would have it no other way. What am I

to believe? At your door my hand

trembles
even before I touch the knob. Inside

you will be on the edge of the bed, I will set
my chair before you, watch

as you show me what it is your body wants,
what word will appear when it's

my hand. We could close our eyes &
wake up almost

anywhere, as if a bird, or birds, had hollowed us
both out. Maybe birds.

MY FEELINGS

                        Maybe I
should be locked in a cage in the center of
the village, a sign

the judge ordered me to carve hung around
my neck

to warn the children of what will happen
if they feed their animals. Go ahead,

use a stick, push the bowl toward me—

if you come close enough I'll tell you
about the years I was faithful, how good

I felt about myself, though she rarely
touched me—by the end we were simply two

abandoned orphans who'd smelled each other
out. These were the years

I believed the body contained the soul, yet
even so I began to feel like

a monster—disgusting, somehow—
until the shadow inside me

became me. I want to say we
really tried but maybe it was simply

the first moment I could be with someone
& say nothing & know

the other understood, or close enough, not be
overcome by my ~~extravagant subterranean~~

~~desperate flimsy shameful crushing guarded~~
~~inappropriate dormant~~

~~backwoods forbidden closeted~~
~~broken limited insubstantial fucked-up wounded~~

~~invisible unspeakable meaningless delicate~~
~~uncontainable elemental filthy~~

~~shallow feral misguided~~
~~distant tethered painful tongue-tied~~

~~wayworn purple~~
~~all-encompassing epic god-given phantom oceanic~~

~~entitled formal flickering~~ feelings.

PUT THE LOAD ON ME

                                        Here, at
your feet, all the gargoyles of heaven—
kneel upon your furnace, their tongues

worship you. You can love only one, the one
you rest your hand upon, his head so

sharp, his sulphur breath . . . . Even now a saint
makes his way up your steps, on his

knees he is coming, he will find you,
with his sword he will kill the beasts, all of them—

he swears this will save you.

    //

Earlier, a deer stood by the side of the road
deciding whether or not to kill me. I cannot

blame her, I cannot blame anyone—many
animals were hurt in the production of this book

just as many trees were hurt & all
the clouds. Open any book

& the cloud above you bursts into
flame, you know this & yet nothing

stops you, the sky stuck to the end of your finger
as you point to it.

   //

This is how it works—the master does not
bow before his servant, he does not

stand naked before her robes, his hands
are empty yet he does not offer—

not even a cupful—of his emptiness,
how could he? How could

the world then keep spinning? He made his money
(as they say) the old-fashioned way, meaning

he earned it, meaning slaves, meaning
go fuck yourself.

   //

Geometry deals with properties of space. Figs
(a "multiple fruit") are like strawberries

only inside-out—its skin is
a receptacle. Saint Francis didn't eat

for forty days, until his body erupted & now
we call it ecstasy. Years later

Frankenstein found a way
to raise the dead. *Friend*, his creation

mutters, *flower.*

    //

A storm will come the radio says find a ditch
& lie facedown in it. Find your ditch & lie

facedown & pray we will all lie down
& pray after all there's only so many places

to hide. We all need help the land is vast
& dense & full of eyes & so many flowers the soil

inside us is darker than oil lie down in it
& pray.

//

Remember: it's not that everything has to look like
something else, or even remind you

of something else—everything
is something else. This is the story

we've been telling ourselves
since we could speak. *Possess*

nothing, Francis says. *Do good*
everywhere. No one believes

those wings will lift you.

POLAROID

He paints her face from memory.
But it doesn't look anything like me, she argues.
Perhaps not, he says—*but it will.*

A NOTE ON THE PERIODIC TABLE

The periodic table names two hundred & twelve elements, or atoms, the so-called *building blocks.* These elements are of a different order than the elements we call fire, air, earth, or water, each of which might be referred to as *archetypal.* Archetypal elements are made up of a combination of atoms, except for fire, which is made only of itself. Or which consumes itself in its very making. One branch of Buddhism claims space & consciousness as elements as well, as elemental as fire, air, earth, etc.. Two hundred & twelve elements—the human body, coincidentally, contains two hundred & twelve bones, half of which are in the hands & feet. What if our purpose as human beings, assuming we have a purpose, is simply to make more of this earth—more dirt—through our shit while we breathe & through our bodies once we stop? Would that be enough to be called *a purpose?* The world is about to run out of gallium, hafnium & indium, but zinc will not disappear until 2037. Zinc is what you take to make you dream. Or, rather, it is used to make your dreams more vivid. Are we really using it all up? What will we do when all the zinc is gone?

HOMILY

Brothers & sisters, the kingdom of
heaven is bought &

sold. Go ahead, punish me,

turn me into salt—it is an act of sanity
to walk by the trees. Sometimes

when I'm home all day I try to remember
to put up the blinds—sunlight

glances off my skin, as if I've stopped on
either side of a two-way mirror—

while outside the hills repeat themselves,
lions, lions, lions, lions, lions, all of us

waiting for the bell to be built
in our blood. Brothers, sometimes

it seems unkind
to keep goldfish in a tank, the body slumped from

midday sun, left breathing its thought—my boy
thinks they're rainbows, he points &

calls them *rainbows* . . . He's stared at himself
too long in the mirror, pride

& satisfaction spread across his face like
oil, across his cheeks like

war paint—still, the face

of any man is the face of all men. Sisters,
sometimes when I'm home all day

I hear what sounds like gunshots
followed by what I can only describe as

a strangled moan. Remember

the story of the tornado, the horses,
framed by the stall window, switched their tails

in darkness. Brothers,
sisters, I want to thank you for how beautifully

your hands move.
We make the world in which we live.

I strap myself to the breaking wheel.
Consider my sin a hymn of praise.

Understanding the miracle, I forget
what it is.

GRAVITY

[five days]

I bring myself to movies in the middle of the day. Today's is about an astronaut—that's all I know, all I want to know. I put on the glasses that make the world real & soon the world is outer space. It starts with a view of the earth—snow over oceans, brown land, all our thoughts from this. A space capsule, drifting in the darkness, some voices—*So what do you like about being up here?* a man asks. A woman answers, *The silence—I could get used to the silence.* For the past five days the phone has rung in the still dark when I am still sleeping. *Your father is in the hospital,* one of the Creole women who takes care of him says, in her beautiful lilt. Soon the astronauts, who are really little more than their voices, are caught in the debris of an exploded satellite & everything falls away from them—their spaceship, the earth, each other. *We can make him comfortable,* the doctor says, *if that's what you decide.* I ask what pills he is on & she lists many, many pills—*To keep the depression out of his spacesuit,* she says.

[meat]

Today, as if answering a question only she could hear, my daughter declared, *I know what little boys are made of—little boys are made of meat.* She looks into my mouth sometimes, says she wants silver teeth like mine. *Why are your teeth silver?* she asks. I want to tell her that there were a few years when I wasn't sure I wanted to be on the planet, until one by one my teeth left me . . .

[diamonds]

That astronaut, when she finally decided to live, her tears floated around our heads like diamonds—my favorite part & I forgot it until just now.

IF THIS IS YOUR FINAL DESTINATION

They say you are made of clouds, they say you
are made of feathers, they say you are everywhere
or nowhere—we know you are both. Our flight
is delayed, this airport another nowhere. *If this
is your final destination,* the air murmurs, *if
a stranger or anyone you do not know well offers you
anything . . .* but how well & what's he offering &
is this our final destination? At the hotel a man
hands us the key to room three one three—home
for a week or so. On the lobby tv a woman once
apparently enormous holds her old jeans up to her
body & smiles. Neil Diamond sings & when I go in-
to the bathroom he follows. *Everybody has one.*
Paradise is cloudless, they say, impossible to know.
Yesterday a man was sucked into the earth as he
slept—a sinkhole opened below his bed—not even
his brother could save him. In the hotel restaurant
my daughter orders corn flakes, they come with a
pitcher of milk, she pours nearly all of it into her bowl,
until I stop her she will keep on pouring. Three more
tvs are screwed into the wall above us—a car goes
round & round, a pitcher throws a baseball, a woman
slams her racket to the clay. My daughter pushes her
bowl away, picks two packets of jelly from the basket,
pulls the plastic off one, then the other, lifts each to
her tongue—red, then purple. The wallpaper is

the texture of trees, a landscape seen from above,
a contour map of an unnamed mountain, people
wandering the face of it. If we were closer we could tell
river from leaf, mountain from shadow, a fire making,
unmaking itself. What is this strand of DNA between
us, unconnected to & of the shadows parading past, our
outlines already chalked into the earth? I live
on air & light, I drag my daughter everywhere,
this morning she muttered *Federer Federer Federer*
like a spell & it was as if he stood before us again, his
perfect red jersey. How many mornings, the sun not yet
up, did I swivel on the red stool at the supermarket
lunch counter, my mother in back extruding donuts,
the aisles dark & empty behind us—she'd bundled me
into the car still sleeping to get there. I'd twirl or
wander or make toast, contemplating the basket
of butter & jelly, each in its little wasteful tub,
impervious to air or time or decay. *Angel of Grape,*
your purple body not only filled those coffins
but took the shape of those coffins—emptiness made
whole, color now a shape. *Angel,* my daughter now
wants only you, she asks for the whole basket, she
pulls back each sheet, puts her tongue in—
strawberry is her favorite, because it tastes
like strawberry.

[five]

ONCE THE ELEPHANT IS GONE

Rats & turnips, pigeons & dogs, we ate
whatever was

left, while the occupiers ate

in restaurants—some of the restaurants
were still

open & near the end

you could order off a "special" menu: zebra, lion,
bear, wildebeest—they were *(of course)*

devouring the zoo & once they ate the elephant,
once the elephant was

gone, they would leave. That's what we
heard. Somehow

you got a box to me—three keys inside
but none

marked. I can now get into every house
you ever lived in, if I could

find the doors, yet you will not be inside, not
any. Somewhere out-

side a child cries, *Come back, come*

back, thinking she can still control her mother's
hands by breathing & maybe

she does, maybe there are no other hands
besides our mother's hands. I'm

not ready to go under, not yet, I'm
clinging to you—

to the idea of you—like an oar
in a dark sea, etc., all of it

true. From my hidey-hole I can see

the street that leads to Termine, the light poles
strung with tiny lights in the shape of

champagne glasses, that somehow even pour
& bubble. I like that it's called

Termine, like the end of something, which
it is.

THE DAY LOU REED DIED

It's not like his songs are going to simply
evaporate,

but since the news I can't stop
listening to him

on endless shuffle—familiar, yes, inside
me, yes, which means

I'm alive, or was, depending on when
you read this. Now

a song called "Sad
Song," the last one on *Berlin*,

sung now from the other side, just talk,
really, at the beginning, then

the promise
or threat, *I'm gonna stop*

wasting my time, but what else
are we made of, especially now? A chorus

sings *Sad song sad song sad song sad*

song. I
knew him better than I knew my own

father, which means
through these songs, which means

not at all. They died on the same day,
what a perfect day, maybe

at the same moment, maybe
both their bodies are laid out now in

the freezer, maybe side by side, maybe
holding hands, waiting

for the fire or the earth or the salt or
the man—

if I could I'd let birds devour whatever's left
& carry them into the sky, but all I can do

it seems
is lie on the couch & shiver, pull a coat

over my body as if it were all I had, as if I
were the one sleeping outside, as if it were my

body something was leaving, rising up
from inside me

& the coat could hold it inside
a little longer.

ALCOHOLISM

Once I fall from my stilts   once the elephant
steps over my body   once the strong man tosses me
& everyone like me into the hay   once I step out of my little car
once the enormous hammer crushes my tiny flowered hat
once I climb the rigging   once I leave the cannon
once sawdust becomes my sea

//

Years later I fell in love with a sword swallower
now when we come to your town we set up in fields
a field like every field   if it rained the night before
it shimmers   pits of shimmer I navigate home
home a trailer on the edge of a field
I hang up my face   she hangs up her sword

//

The ferris wheel stops at the top
to let someone on   I sway in my chair
the tent is staked to the earth below
I used my hammer like everyone else
I am the one shot out of the cannon
each day at three   this same face
this same cigarette   a tiny ember
I'm always on fire   I end the fucken show

MOFUKU

Waking in the middle of the night, wandering room to room in a black t-shirt in a house that is not your own, looking for something you know isn't there. A few days later I will tell my daughter he is gone & she will turn it over inside her for a moment. Then she will announce, *So both your mom & your dad are skeletons now . . .*

THE INCOMPREHENSIBILITY

The newly dead hung on to the ceiling last night
>   like moths, wanting to tell us what they hadn't
>   found words for yet, their bodies still

warm on their mattresses below—they did not look
>   comfortable, passing themselves on the way
>   out . . . *Only mystery allows us*

to live—Lorca wrote this on the back of one of his many
>   drawings of a sailor, or of many sailors. *Only*
>   *mystery* & yet or so

I pull myself back again to a place wherein I can *com-*
>   *prehend*, if only a glimmer, the moment my mother
>   will press a bullet into the chamber of her .38—

think of Fra Angelico's *Annunciation*—nothing has happened,
>   not yet, Mary's back is to the Angel, his hand
>   hovers over her shoulder, not touching her, not

yet. It's still not too late to turn back—a Sunday morning,
>   we can hear the ocean, we can smell it, if we could get up
>   we could even see it. Junkies

can go to a clinic in downtown Vancouver now to shoot up
>   in safety—*We can help them find*
>   *the vein*, the pretty nurse says,

but we cannot depress the plunger . . . As I write this a Boeing 777

along with all two hundred & thirty-nine souls onboard

vanishes from the sky—

no distress call, no black box, no wreckage. By the time you

read this we will all know what happened (wormhole?

drunk pilot?) but right now it is simply

gone. Let's look again at the *Annunciation,* let's think of

the angel as a pretty nurse, let's think of her wings as

possibility, her silence

as a syringe. Let's put my mother in that airplane now, let's

let her circle forever, let's imagine she too is unable to

land. She glances out the window, sometimes

at the tops of the clouds, sometimes at someone's sad house

below. *I know you're still in there,* she whispers, raising one

finger. *Poke a hole through the heavy curtains,* she

mouths—*you'll see they are not even real.*

THE WASHING OF THE BODY

Blood carries oxygen & each muscle
                hungers for it

      a fluorescent stutters above your head
I don't understand   then I do

gasp to gasp I hold on to your hand   as you
              become air &

        after a while we get hungry &
    we ride the elevator down & after a while

            you stop

   //

        Marie: *What happens now?*
        Nurse: *First we wash the body,*
                then we send him downstairs.
        Marie: *Can we be the ones to wash him—*
            I mean, can the men?

   //

Twenty years I've tried to write this
      only to end up

this isn't it, this isn't it

here

                //

Again:

                        your mother
as we came off the elevator

her palm on your door

                        Marie tells us
a pure light filled the room   tells us

                we would be the ones
            that we would be the ones to wash you

the door behind us closes

            //

in Prague a year earlier I'd
        stood before a mural at the Jewish

Cemetery—twelve

panels, a body passed
    from deathbed to grave

one panel titled
    The Washing of the Body

    & three men stood around him
& each held a cloth

    //

The light dimmed now   no one knows how
        to begin

then one finds a pan & fills it   then one floats
    a small bar of soap

one says   *I've never seen a body*
one says   *I've never touched one*

A dead one   one laughs   *He's still here*
    one says

    one calls you *sweetie*

we each take a cloth   *Billy,*
we're going to wash you now,

            Billy, sweetheart

        //

I tried to write about the blizzard
how it stranded me after we'd scattered
                your ash

my truck *(remember?)*—your tv, your
chair, your rug—nothing made it

            to the city, I abandoned it all
in the snow

        //

The hair on your thigh mats beneath
                    my hand

faint blue your lips   your nostrils caked

one strokes your forehead
        one spreads your toes

He's in good shape   one says

        No wasting   one says

  //

The ring on your finger

           soap won't release it

it's almost too late

          you can almost not hear

once we untie your johnnie the ring is all

that isn't you

one whispers   *Sweetie,*

we're going to roll you over now

your back

still warm where the blood pools

PHILIP SEYMOUR HOFFMAN

Last summer I found a small box stashed away in my apartment, a box filled with enough Vicodin to kill me. I would have sworn that I'd thrown it away years earlier, but apparently not. I stared at the white pills blankly for a long while, I even took a picture of them, before (finally, definitely) throwing them away. I'd been sober (again) for some years when I found that box, but every addict has one—a little box, metaphoric or actual—hidden away. Before I flushed them I held them in my palm, marveling that at some point in the not-so-distant past it seemed a good idea to keep a stash of pills on hand. *For an emergency*, I told myself. What kind of emergency? What if I needed a root canal on a Sunday night? This little box would see me through until the dentist showed up for work the next morning. Half my brain told me that, while the other half knew that looking into that box was akin to seeing a photograph of myself standing on the edge of a bridge, a bridge in the familiar dark neighborhood of my mind, that comfortable place where I could somehow believe that *fuck it* was an adequate response to life.

THE BOOK OF ASH

Half-burnt, half-
buried, abandoned in a dark pit

dug out of sand—*a book*—beach chairs
all around it. No one else seemed to

even notice. That beach,
that spot—I read *Of Mice & Men* there,

years ago, a worn-out paperback,
so worn the glue was brittle, so

brittle each

page pulled free from the spine
as I turned it. A windy day, each

page blew from my hand, skittered off
down the beach until

the last page . . . Now, on my desk, *The Book
of Ash*, ash fallen

to the floor around us. I ask my daughter
not to touch it but of course she

touches it, her fingertips black now. The spine
is burnt completely away, it burned

from the top down, the spine like a fuse, the flame
running down it while fanning

upward. Now, when I open what's left
it looks like wings. From what can be

deciphered it was a test, or maybe

simply a way to prepare for a test—pages
of stories

followed by pages of questions, the answers
multiple choice. A drawing of some

leaves, the answers on the facing page:
       a: burned b: holes c: displayed

                         Now,
when you open what's left, ash falls like

tiny black feathers. Hold this wing up
to the light, the carbon letters

shine. *Be. Fifteen. Was.* This is how flames
will paraphrase us all.

This book, this ash. I try to pull it back
together, I glue each wing

into a clean white book.

FORTY-SEVEN MINUTES

I ask a high school class to locate an image in a poem we've just read—their heads at this moment are bowed to the page. After some back & forth about the rain & a styrofoam cup, a girl raises her hand & asks, *Does it matter?* I smile—it's as if the universe was balanced on those three words & we've landed in the unanswerable & I have to admit that no, it doesn't, not really, matter, if rain is an image or rain is an idea or rain is a sound in our heads. *But to get through the next forty-seven minutes we might have to pretend it does.*

EPITHALAMION

No one—

not the wind in the leaves, not
the leaves in the sky—can promise

permanence, no one

gets all the days, even if it seems
that we are the ones

writing the book, even if it seems

that we are the ones
who made each leaf. Inside each leaf

more leaves, inside these trees

more trees, some so old they threaten
the roof, some so tiny we will need

to keep the deer from them. Each leaf is not
a word, each branch not

a sentence, yet

the wind *is* saying something—*inevitable?*
unlikely?—even if impossible to

perfectly translate. Now imagine these trees
as a roomful of books, each

book spills from its stack—remember

each hour alone, reciting the alphabet,
marveling at how the letters cluster, how each

comes with its mouthful of sound—until
a word somehow

entered you. One morning you will turn

toward whomever is laying beside you
& ask, *Why do I feel*

I am falling into the center of the earth? That

same morning you will reach your hand up
& know it will be caught. What were you

before this?

MARATHON

                    Petals
on a river, a tree in blossom, one
pink bud—unopened—falls

& is carried downstream & out
to sea. From

above the other petals seem to
carry it. Closer—

this is our map, these our
footprints, we

grew up drinking this water. At the
start there

was doubt, we lit a torch, no one
believed we would

make it. Closer—

the legs, the heart, the lungs. It's
too soon to say

we were lucky, it's too soon to say
anything,

until the cloud is pulled back
from the sky, until the ringing is

pulled back from the bells. Look—
everyone we've ever known

runs without thinking
not away but *into* the cloud, where we are

waiting.

[some notes]

YOU CANNOT FOLD A FLOOD . . .
the epigraph that begins the book is from emily dickinson, 214 (530).

AK-47
a pecha kucha starting with a line from jack gilbert *(love lays hold of everything)*, followed by a line from jorge luis borges *(what need is there to build a labyrinth when the entire universe is one?)*, a reference to the film *memento,* a line from herakles via anne carson *(to love the dead is endless tears),* a line (approximately) from bj (the chicago kid), from the song "his pain," *(I don't know why god keeps blessing me),* & ending with a line from roscoe mitchell *(only silence is perfect)*—thanks to terrance hayes for introducing many of us to the pecha kucha form. AK-47 was first presented by musiqa in *frozen time,* a performance organized by anthony brandt as a collaboration with composers elena firsova, karim al-zand, lei liang & marcus karl maroney (asia society texas center, houston, 2014)—it was inspired by janos sugar's film *typewriter of the illiterate,* which screened at the station museum in houston (2010), in a show curated by jim harithas.

TANTULUS
for mark conway on his fiftieth birthday.

BEADS OF SWEAT
the title is borrowed from the laura nyro album.

MY TRIGGERS
the phrase *as indispensible as oxygen for the body* is jung's.

WHEN I WAS A GIRL
written for the anthology *the mind of monticello: 50 contemporary poets on thomas jefferson* (university of virginia press, 2016). *note:*

in a private letter (1803) to william henry harrison, regarding his views on native americans, thomas jefferson wrote:

> To promote this disposition to exchange lands, which they have to spare and we want, for necessaries, which we have to spare and they want, we shall push our trading uses, and be glad to see the good and influential individuals among them run in debt, because we observe that when these debts get beyond what the individuals can pay, they become willing to lop them off by a cession of lands. . . . In this way our settlements will gradually circumscribe and approach the Indians, and they will in time either incorporate with us as citizens of the United States, or remove beyond the Mississippi. The former is certainly the termination of their history most happy for themselves; but, in the whole course of this, it is essential to cultivate their love. As to their fear, we presume that our strength and their weakness is now so visible that they must see we have only to shut our hand to crush them, and that all our liberalities to them proceed from motives of pure humanity only. Should any tribe be foolhardy enough to take up the hatchet at any time, the seizing the whole country of that tribe, and driving them across the Mississippi, as the only condition of peace, would be an example to others, and a furtherance of our final consolidation.

HARBOR
based on a still from a mischa richter short film.

MY BLINDNESS
1 Sam. 25:34; 1 Kings 14:10; 21:21.

PUT THE LOAD ON ME
written as a collaboration with mel chin for his installation *funk & wag a to z,* published in a limited edition art book (menil press, 2014), edited by helen nagge, designed by susan rhew.

POLAROID
the exchange is between picasso & stein *[approximately]*.

HOMILY
a cento made up of lines gathered from poems by josh gottlieb-miller, jennifer lowe, caitlin plunkett, nicole walker, michelle oakes, allie rowbottom & patrick james.

GRAVITY
inspired in part by the film *gravity*.

THE DAY LOU REED DIED
borrows phrases from various lou reed songs.

THE INCOMPREHENSIBILITY
borrows a gesture from james tate's "the lost pilot" & was inspired in part by alejandro gonzález iñárritu's film *biutiful*.

THE WASHING OF THE BODY
for michael cunningham, micheal klein, marie howe, & billy forlenza *(r.i.p.)*.

EPITHALAMION
written for the wedding of bill clegg & van scott, 2013.

MARATHON
written in response to the boston marathon bombing, 2013.

[debts]

deep thanks offered to the following editors & organizations that helped shepherd these poems into existence—the atlantic center for the arts, katie dublinski, fiona mccrae, eireann lorsung, paul muldoon, don share, elizabeth scanlon, corey zeller, rob spillman, matthew dickman, nate nakadate, alex dimitrov, january gill o'neill, sven birkerts, tara bray, memye curtis tucker, lisa russ spaar, david weisberg, carrie moniz, jason schwartz, koshin paley ellison, kasia florinovich, david bonanno, ashley peel, jon thompson, meg storey, dominic luxford, jim frost, david baker, ladette randolph, akshay ahuja, the fine arts work center

as well as those who continually sustain me—lili taylor, bill clegg, tom "tojo" johnston, claudia rankine, john lucas, j kastely, michael klein, mark conway, jacqueline woodson, rachel eliza griffiths, fady joudah, stephen elliott, john bowe, alix lambert, mel chin, ronnie yates, kelle groom, gabriel martinez, garrett burrell, lulu sylbert, lisa lucas, hubert sauper, annalia luna, alison granucci, rick moody, jill bialosky, nuar alsadir, robert curry, anne carson, sophie klahr, tony swofford, wayne gilbert, lacy johnson, greg pardlo, ed hirsch, olena kalytiak davis, beth bachmann, jared handelsman, suzanne gardinier, robert chodo campbell, carolyn forché, william middleton, layla benitez-james, richard mccann, mary ruefle, tony hoagland, mat johnson, matthew zapruder, elee kraljii gardiner, ivan coyote, melissa febos, david brody, karen farber, guy barash, fred marchant, tad flynn, maeve lulu taylor flynn

these poems first appeared in the following publications—miel, american poetry review, the california journal of poetics, agni, ampersand, the academy of american poets (poem-a-day), poetry, atlanta review, death hums, fugue, story houston, tin house, the new yorker, the rumpus, gigantic sequins, boston magazine, tricycle, free verse: a journal of contemporary poetry & poetics, the kenyon review, ploughshares

[the author]

Nick Flynn has worked as a ship's captain, an electrician, and as a case-worker with homeless adults. For the past ten years he has been a professor on the creative writing faculty of the University of Houston, where he is in residence each spring. Otherwise, he lives in or near Brooklyn.

www.nickflynn.org

The text of *My Feelings* is set in Giovanni, a typeface designed by Robert Slimbach. Book design by Ann Sudmeier. Composition by Bookmobile Design & Digital Publisher Services, Minneapolis, Minnesota. Manufactured by Versa Press on acid-free, 30 percent postconsumer wastepaper.